Sally's Spaceship

Written by Susan McCloskey Illustrated by Esther Szegedy

"I want to see the stars!" said Sally.

So Sally made a spaceship.
Sally got a box.

Sally got some string.
Sally worked a long time.

"You will need to eat," said Mom.

"I will take a snack," said Sally.

"You will need to sleep," said Mom.

"I will take a pillow," said Sally.

"You will need a friend," said Mom.

"I will take Spot," said Sally.

"I made a spaceship so I can see the stars!"

"Good-bye, Mom," said Sally.

14

So Sally saw the stars.